Animal Classifications

Amphibians

Angela Royston

raintree

a Capstone company — publishers for children

Raintree is an imprint of Capstone Global Library Limited, a company incorporated in England and Wales having its registered office at 7 Pilgrim Street, London, EC4V 6LB – Registered company number: 6695582

www.raintree.co.uk
myorders@raintree.co.uk

Text © Capstone Global Library Limited 2015
The moral rights of the proprietor have been asserted.

Edited by Helen Cox Cannons, Clare Lewis
    and Abby Colich
Designed by Steve Mead
Picture research by Tracy Cummins
Production by Victoria Fitzgerald
Originated by Capstone Global Library Ltd
Printed and bound in China

ISBN 978 1 406 28736 3
18 17 16 15 14
10 9 8 7 6 5 4 3 2 1

British Library Cataloguing in Publication Data
A full catalogue record for this book is available from the British Library.

Acknowledgements
We would like to thank the following for permission to reproduce photographs: Alamy: © ephotocorp, 7, 28; Getty Images: Peter Ptschelinzew, 26, Thomas Marent, 15, 29 Bottom; Shutterstock: Artur Synenko, 4, Designua, 12, Dirk Ercken, Cover, Dr. Morley Read, 21, Durden Images, 22, Eduard Kyslynskyy, 8, Ian Grainger, 14, Kazakov Maksim, 18, Marek R. Swadzba, 23, 29 Middle, Martin Fowler, 10, Matt Jeppson, 9, 27, Nashepard, 5, Pan Xunbin, Design Element, Paul Broadbent, 13, Peter Reijners, 24, reptiles4all, 25, WitR, 6; SuperStock: Animals Animals, 19, Minden Pictures, 16, 17, 29 Top, NHPA, 11, 20.

We would like to thank Michael Bright for his invaluable help in the preparation of this book.

Every effort has been made to contact copyright holders of material reproduced in this book. Any omissions will be rectified in subsequent printings if notice is given to the publisher.

Contents

Some words are shown in bold, **like this.** You can find
out what they mean by looking in the glossary.

Meet the amphibians

Scientists divide living things into groups. This is called **classification**. The animals in each group have certain things in common. One group is called the amphibians. Most amphibians spend part of their lives in water and part on land.

A frog is at home in water as well as on land.

A salamander is a type of amphibian.

Amphibians are part of a larger group called **vertebrates**. All vertebrates have a **backbone** and a hard **skeleton** inside their bodies. Birds, reptiles and mammals are also vertebrates.

Body shape

Amphibians are divided into three groups. You can tell which group an amphibian belongs to by the shape of its body. Adult frogs and toads have four legs and no tail. Salamanders and newts have four legs and a tail.

Some male newts have a crest along their back and a colourful belly.

Caecilians live in hot, wet places in the **tropics**.

Caecilians have no legs and look a bit like worms. Most caecilians also **burrow** through the soil. Unlike worms, caecilians have bones and teeth.

On the move

Different amphibians move in different ways. Frogs and toads have **webbed feet**, which help them to swim fast through water. Most use their long back legs to hop over the ground.

When a frog is in danger, it quickly leaps to safety.

A salamander's legs are so short that its belly drags on the ground.

Salamanders and newts have short legs and squirm from side to side as they walk. Some amphibians spend most of their time in the water. They swim or crawl along the bottom of streams.

Warming up

Amphibians are **cold blooded**. This means that they cannot make their own body heat, as birds and mammals do. Instead, they take in warmth from the sun and their surroundings.

A frog warms up in the daytime and cools off at night.

Frogs sleep through the winter in underground burrows.

The warmer an amphibian becomes, the faster it moves about. In winter, when the weather is very cold, amphibians slow down. Many dig a **burrow** and **hibernate** during the winter.

Changing shape

Most amphibians begin life as **tadpoles**. The tadpoles look very different from the adult amphibians. A tadpole **hatches** from an egg, which its mother laid in water. A tadpole looks a bit like a tiny fish.

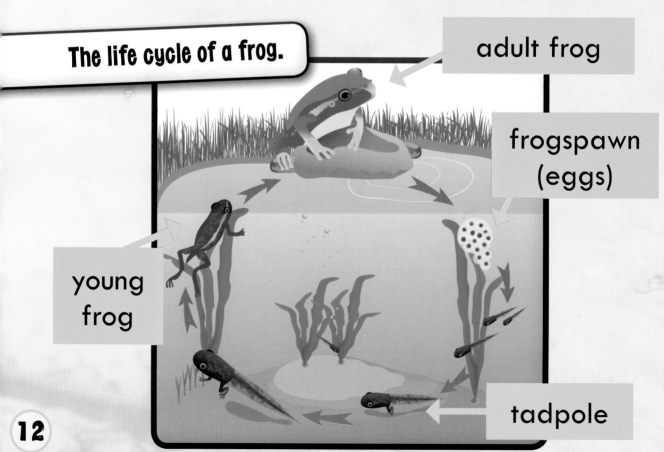

The life cycle of a frog.

adult frog

frogspawn (eggs)

young frog

tadpole

Tadpoles feed on plants in the water as they grow.

As the tadpoles grow bigger, their bodies change. Some grow legs, and their tails become shorter. This change is called **metamorphosis**.

Masses of eggs

Some amphibians lay thousands of eggs. The eggs float in the water in a mass of jelly called **spawn**. The tiny **tadpoles** grow bigger and bigger until they are ready to **hatch**.

Each black blob in this frogspawn will be a tiny tadpole. One by one the tadpoles will hatch from the eggs.

A male midwife toad carries the eggs on his body until they hatch.

Many of the eggs are eaten by fish and other animals. Some amphibians, such as the midwife toad, lay fewer eggs and look after them until they hatch.

Tadpoles

A **tadpole** is at home in the water. It uses its long tail for swimming, and it breathes through its **gills**. However, many tadpoles do not survive, because they are eaten by fish and other animals.

At first, salamander tadpoles have feathery gills, but soon the gills are hidden under the skin.

gills

legs

This tadpole has grown its first pair of legs.

When a tadpole is about five weeks old, its legs begin to grow. With frogs, the back legs grow first. With salamanders, the front legs are the first to grow.

Never grow up

Most **tadpoles** grow **lungs** so that they can breathe air. However, some salamanders keep their **gills** all their lives.

An axolotl has pink gills and spends its whole life in water.

gills

A mudpuppy grows to about 28 centimetres (11 inches) long.

Axolotls, mudpuppies and sirens stay a bit like tadpoles all their lives. They never leave the water, and live mostly at the bottom of ponds and streams. You can tell which ones are sirens because they have only two legs.

Becoming an adult

After a **tadpole** has grown one pair of legs, the second pair grows. A froglet's tail becomes shorter as it grows. However, salamanders keep their tails.

As its tail gets shorter, the growing frog uses its legs and **webbed feet** to swim.

This tiny frog is sitting on a leaf that floats on the water.

When it is 12 or more weeks old, the frog or salamander leaves the water and climbs on to a leaf or twig. It stays close to the water, ready to jump back in.

Slippery skin

Amphibians have very thin skin. Their skin is so thin that water can move through it. This means that an amphibian has to keep its skin damp. Otherwise, the inside of its body would dry out.

Most amphibians live in damp places so that their skin does not dry out.

This salamander is brightly coloured to warn attackers that it is poisonous.

An amphibian's skin is covered with thick, slimy liquid, called **mucus**. Some amphibians have poisonous skins, which help defend against attackers.

Tree frogs

Tree frogs live high above the ground in **tropical** rainforests. The air is so damp, their skin never dries out. They lay their eggs in pools of rainwater that collect in the leaves.

Tree frogs have special pads on their feet to help them cling to plants.

A golden dart frog is the most poisonous amphibian of all.

Some tree frogs defend themselves from attack by making poison in their skin. The poison from the most poisonous frogs can even kill a human.

One incredible amphibian!

Amphibians need to live in damp places, but a few amazing frogs live in hot deserts. They survive by **burrowing** into the ground and waiting until it rains.

Australia's Great Sandy Desert is usually very dry, but sometimes it rains very hard.

This frog spends ten months of the year hiding in its burrow.

When they hear rain, the frogs come to the surface and lay eggs. The eggs **hatch** and the **tadpoles** develop very quickly. Just over two weeks later, the new frogs are ready to dig their own **burrow.**

Quiz

Look at the pictures and read the clues. Can you remember the names of these amphibians? Look back in the book if you need help.

1. I look like a worm. I live in hot places. What am I?

2. I am a young frog. What am I called?

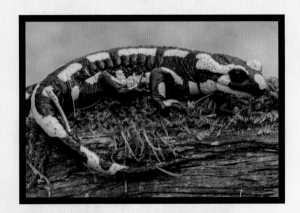

3. I have four legs and a tail. I can have very bright skin. What am I?

4. I carry my eggs on my back until they are ready to **hatch.** What am I?

Glossary

backbone row of knobbly bones in the back

burrow animal's underground home; to dig an underground home

classification system that scientists use to divide living things into separate groups

cold blooded when an animal is unable to make its own heat and has to take heat from its surroundings

gills body part that allows amphibians to take in the gas oxygen from water

hatch break out of an egg

hibernate go into a very deep sleep to survive very cold or very dry weather

lungs parts of the body that allow animals to take in the gas oxygen from the air when the animal breathes in

metamorphosis complete change in body shape that amphibians go through when the young become adults

mucus thick, slippery liquid made by the body

skeleton hard, bony frame inside the body. It is the skeleton that gives vertebrate animals their shape.

spawn mass of eggs held together by jelly

tadpole young stage of being an amphibian

tropical used to describe a plant, bird or rainforest found in the tropics

tropics places with hot, steamy weather

vertebrates animals that have a backbone and skeleton inside their bodies

webbed feet feet that have a layer of skin that stretches between the toes

Find out more

Books

Amphibian Babies, Catherine Veitch (Raintree, 2014)

Amphibians (True or False), Melvin and Gilda Berger (Scholastic, 2011)

Reptiles and Amphibians (Deadly Factbook), Steve Backshall (Orion Books, 2013)

Websites

www.bbc.co.uk/nature/life/Amphibian

Find out lots of fascinating information about amphibians.

kids.sandiegozoo.org/animals/amphibians

The kids' section of the San Diego Zoo website includes photos and information about amphibians. Click on the small photos to find out about particular animals. Don't miss the games, videos and animal cams at the top.

Index